MAXIMISE YOUR TIME !

Forthcoming titles in this series will include

- *Winning Negotiation Tactics!*
- *Painless Business Finance*
- *Planning your Business*
- *Winning CVs!*
- *Getting Hired!*
- *Managing People for the First Time*
- *Successful Interviewing Techniques*
- *Letter Writing for Winners*
- *Winning Telephone Techniques*
- *Effective Appraisal Skills*

Do you have ideas for subjects which could be included in this exciting and innovative series? Could your company benefit from close involvement with a forthcoming title?

Please write to David Grant Publishing Limited
80 Ridgeway, Pembury, Tunbridge Wells, Kent TN2 4EZ
with your ideas or suggestions.

Ronald Bracey

60 Minutes Success Skills Series

First published 1997 by
David Grant Publishing Limited
80 Ridgeway, Pembury, Kent TN2 4EZ United Kingdom
99 98 97   10 9 8 7 6 5 4 3 2 1

60 Minutes Success Skills Series is an imprint of
David Grant Publishing Limited

British Library Cataloguing in Publication Data
A CIP catalogue record for this book is available from the British Library

ISBN 1-901306-02-X

Cover design: Steve Haynes

Text design: Graham Rich

Production editor: Paul Stringer

Typeset in Futura by
Archetype, Stow-on-the-Wold
http://ourworld/compuserve.com/homepages/Archetype

Printed and bound in Great Britain by
T.J. Press Ltd, Padstow, Cornwall

This book is printed on acid-free paper

CONTENTS

Welcome: *About Maximise Your Time!*   7

Chapter 1: Understanding time – what is it?   11
Time thieves
Learning from others
The economic value of time
Physical and psychological time
What's stopping you from using your time well?
How to improve your understanding of time

Chapter 2: Analysing where time goes   21
Dissect a typical day
Realistic ambition
The Pareto Principle
Free lunches
Understand where all of your time goes

Chapter 3: Do it now, not tomorrow   27
Time cancer
Write lists
The fear factor
Working when the muse is with you
How to get it done, now

Chapter 4: Saving time at work   37
Define what is expected of you
Homework
Hell is other people
Meetings
Telephone techniques
Unexpected guests
Delegating, not passing the buck
Tips on saving time at work

Chapter 5: Get organised and feel good   **47**
Setting priorities
Just-in-case hoarding
Your desk
Managing information
Effective writing
Filling in the gaps
Time-saving technology
How to organise your work life

ABOUT *MAXIMISE YOUR TIME!*

Can you learn to maximise the use of your time in just one hour? The answer is a resounding "Yes".

The only bit of waffle in this book

The 60 Minutes Success Skills Series is for people with neither the time nor patience to trawl through acres of jargon. If you want to avoid management-speak and page-filling waffle, this book is definitely for you.

Like all books in the series, *Maximise Your Time!* has been written in the belief that you can learn all you really need to know quickly and without fuss. The aim is to provide essential, practical advice that you can use straight away. This book is a tool to help you change your behaviour.

The following chapters explain to you simple, yet effective ways of literally extending your life. You can learn from them how to get the utmost from the available time you have. Each day will take on a new meaning and life itself will become a new and fulfilling challenge.

Is this book for you?

Maximise Your Time! is for those people who never seem to have enough time. Do you recognise any of these symptoms?

- ○ *Your life is one big panic.*
- ○ *Your life seems to be speeding past without you getting anywhere.*
- ○ *You seem to waste so much time at home and at work.*
- ○ *Life is so stressful – there's no time to catch up.*
- ○ *You always seem to miss deadlines.*
- ○ *You have dreams and ambitions, but never the time to pursue them.*

If you identify with any of these statements, then this is the book for you.

Why is maximising time important?

Quite simply, if you are not in control of your time, you can never be fully in control of your life. Without good time management you will be:

○ *inefficient – or, perhaps as important, seen to be inefficient;*
○ *unfulfilled – you will never be able to achieve your potential;*
○ *passed over for promotion – missed deadlines and the air of panic around you will not inspire confidence in your abilities;*
○ *stressed – you will not enjoy your work and your worries will spill over into your personal life.*

A lack of control could even be job-threatening. Businesses these days will not tolerate poor-performers so you might become a target for redundancy.

If you apply the techniques described in this book you will learn how to prioritise tasks and start them immediately, delegate effectively, manage your boss and organise your work life. You will then regain mastery over where your time goes, which in turn will allow you to:

○ *spend more time doing the things you want to do;*
○ *leave your worries at work and improve your home life;*
○ *enjoy better relationships with your colleagues;*
○ *give your best and feel fully satisfied with your contribution.*

Remember, time management skills can be learnt and applied quickly. There's nothing to stop you improving your quality of life.

How to use this book

The message in this book is: "It's OK to skim." Feel free to flick through to find the help you most need. The book is a collection of "hands on" tips that will help you organise your precious time in the way that suits you best. *Maximise Your Time!* is a guide to dip into for ideas and help. You do not have to read it all at one go or do everything advised straight away.

You will find that there are some graphic features used throughout the book:

This means "Something to think about" – it sets the scene and identifies the problems by prompting you to think about situations which will instantly feel familiar.

With the problem diagnosed, these features give you the framework for an action plan – this will help you to get your own ideas in order.

This feature appears at the end of each chapter. It is a checklist which condenses all of the advice given throughout the chapter. Similar features also appear within chapters which are overflowing with tips!

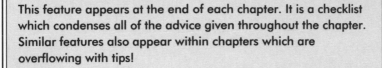

As you read through the chapters, you will come across lots of tips and practical advice on how to make the most of your time. You could start by just going straight to any of the graphic features, which will ask you to either think about a problem or to do something about it and give you some ideas. If you're really pushed for time, you can always go direct to the tips features and the end of each chapter. These are also a useful reminder when you come back to look at this book in the future.

Good luck.

What's in this chapter for you

Accounting for how you use your time

Why some tasks seem to take an eternity

Have a greater sense of achievement at the end of the day

Feel that you are starting to get your priorities right

> " *Men talk of killing time while time quietly kills them . . .* "
> **– Dion Boucicault, Irish playwright**

> " *To say I have bad days at work is an understatement. There seem to be times when I go into the office, rush around all day, and achieve nothing apart from sending my stress level through the roof. Then I go home and do it all over again next day.* "
> **– Diane Little, financial consultant**

Time thieves

Forget gold and diamonds, time is the most precious commodity of all. You have just one chance to achieve your dreams and ambitions, one chance to live life to the full. You need to start thinking about your relationship with time now.

By spending your time gardening, reading the newspaper or watching television, you are sacrificing opportunities to do a whole range of other things. Simply staying in bed for an extra 15 minutes in the morning, every day of your life, will add up to months of waking life lost for ever.

Think of the following daily activities and how much time you will spend on them cumulatively throughout your life:

❑ *Watching the TV news for 30 minutes every day takes up about 18 months of active life!*

❑ *Commuting to work an hour each way over a working life loses you two and a half years !*

Spending time commuting is, alas, an unfortunate fact of life. However, what do you do with that time on the train or in the car? If you are in effect wasting it, then in reality you could be losing up to three years of your life.

Some time management theories state that the television is the devil's handiwork and that you should stop watching altogether. This seems a little extreme. Try to ration what you watch – if you are into sport or documentaries, or even soaps, reward yourself with a little quality viewing when you feel you need it. But be in control and avoid the couch potato syndrome – don't watch TV for the sake of it!

How can you use these pockets of fragmented time usefully? How can you learn to use your time to achieve greater success at work and greater happiness at home?.

Look at your typical working day and how simple changes in your routine could save you valuable minutes. Add your own examples.

	saving per day	savings per week
Get up at 7 am instead of 7.30	30 minutes	2.5 hours
Refuse to bring work home	30 minutes	2.5 hours
Read routine reports on the train	90 minutes	7.5 hours
Avoid unproductive weekly meetings	30 minutes	2.5 hours

❑

❑

❑

Hey presto, we've just saved over 15 hours in one week! However, this is only a real saving if you can use these 15 hours for something else you really value.

What would you do with the extra time?

- *You could lock yourself in your study and start writing the novel you've been waiting to unleash.*
- *You could learn a new language, start an MBA course or study for a professional qualification.*
- *You may wish to invest in getting fit, mastering a new sport or going to night school.*

> **❝** *I had never been taught to swim properly when I was young. Family holidays became an embarrassment when my children overtook me with ease in the swimming pool and laughed at my uncoordinated attempts to swim a length! An eight-week course at the local baths means that they still beat me, but at least I swim with dignity! Plus, regular swimming keeps me fit and gives me so much more energy.* **❞**
> **– Julie Morgan, social worker**

> Identify those chunks of time that produce nothing for you and decide where you can make instant savings. Set yourself some goals, whether at work or at home, and decide to spend time doing things that *you* want to do.

Learning from others

Everything you think and do can be done differently. Some people spend their lives at the cutting edge, squeezing out each and every drop of pleasure and achievement. These people are usually very successful, contented and happy.

> **❝** *I can never work out why my days are spent in a total panic while my boss and other members of the team always seem to be on top of the job.* **❞**
> **– Jill Cavendish, production controller**

Really successful people have mastered the art of managing time. Time is their slave. All they have done is to have learnt to harness some simple straightforward rules of life.

Social learning is one of the keys to change. People learn from watching each other. This is called vicarious learning. We all experience this from the earliest age. Small children are attentive – they watch every move, listen to every sound and slowly build up an understanding of the social world around them. Unfortunately, a lot of us seem to be best at learning bad habits and becoming time-bound, a slave to the clock.

> **Some people use the whole 24 hours to work, play and to live life to the full. What is stopping you from doing the same?**

If you're in the company of successful people you will often start to behave in the same way as they do. You may actually learn successful behaviour from copying the habits of those people who have achieved what you aspire to.

> **Think of five people you admire and respect for their efficiency – list the attributes that you think give them an edge.**
>
> ❑
>
> ❑
>
> ❑

If you are unsure what is giving them that edge, ask them!

- ○ *How do they use their free time?*
- ○ *Are they good delegators?*
- ○ *Do they cut through paperwork?*
- ○ *Do their meetings run to time?*
- ○ *How do they deal with time-wasters?*
- ○ *How do they stay in control of their work and so well organised?*
- ○ *How did they learn all of this?*

> ❝ *I had been on a variety of time management courses but had never had the time to implement what I had learnt! During an assessment, I asked my boss how she always seemed to achieve so much in the same working day. I learnt more from watching and listening to her than all the courses put together.* ❞
> **– Pete Reynolds, insurance agent**

Change your life by changing your habits.

- ❏ *Learn good practice from those around you that you respect.*
- ❏ *Identify regular unproductive time and change the routine.*
- ❏ *Set goals for what you want to achieve in the time saved.*

The economic value of time

Your time obviously has an economic value which can be translated into a real cost and you must be aware of what it is.

Take an average annual salary, for instance £20,000. Assuming an average working day of eight hours, you'll receive (after various stoppages) approximately £10 for every hour you spend at work. Now think of what you hope the money you earn will pay for you to do. Have you booked your holiday? A £400 summer holiday could be paid for by next Monday morning!

What do you earn in one hour? How many of the activities you find yourself involved in merit you earning that amount of money? Put the time that you spend at work into perspective. By thinking of what you are achieving in monetary terms, you can motivate yourself to work more efficiently.

It may seem outlandish to look at time in this way but it lets you put a money value on whatever you do. If you are trying to make the point to your manager that there's no reason for you to waste your life in the weekly waffle meeting, telling him or her what it's costing to have you present will go a long way towards securing your liberation. Anything unproductive could be costing you more than just money – your time.

> *" My partner and I were six months into our new, low-overhead business. One day, after having stuffed envelopes for our freelance sales team since 9.30 a.m., I looked at the clock and realised it was 4 o'clock in the afternoon! We had done nothing creative or developmental all day, but had wasted £250 pounds in executive salaries for stuffing envelopes! And we still had our regular day's work to do. Two weeks later, we recruited a sales office assistant. "*
> **– Richard Allen, publisher**

Make the most of your time – know its worth.

❑ *Calculate your hourly salary – strive to give value for money all of the time.*
❑ *Avoid false economies – do the work that you are paid to do.*

Physical and psychological time

> *" All my possessions for a moment of time. "*
> **– Queen Elizabeth I**

An atomic clock can set the time to an accuracy of a trillionth of a second. This is all well and good but time still relentlessly ticks away second by second, hour by hour, and there's nothing we can do about it. We measure everything against this absolute time. We reset ourselves every time we look at a clock. Physical time dominates most of us.

Does a ten minute wait at the dentist seem to last for hours?. Did the last exam that you sat fly by in seconds? Does the day at work disappear without you having achieved anything?

Yes, time does play tricks on us. Jet lag is a good example. What about when you drop off to sleep for what seems like a few moments and then you realise with horror that about 7 hours have past? You feel severely cheated!

> Realise that time will never behave uniformly for you. Your day may have passed quickly, and you may even have enjoyed it, but did you achieve what you wanted or had to? Are you storing up problems for yourself tomorrow? Analyse your day.

Awaiting execution, a condemned man may perceive five minutes as a lifetime. A person with a low boredom threshold stuck in a seemingly endless departmental meeting may perceive it as a lifetime of misery.

> ❝ When I started running sales, I inherited a system whereby all the sales team came into the office once a month. We had a nice lunch and it was great fun, but what were we achieving? I decided to cancel these get-togethers and now ensure that I go out with each rep once a month to see key customers. ❞
> **– Terry Menges, sales manager**

What's stopping you from using your time well?

You must elevate controlling time to its appropriate level of importance – it should be at the top of your priorities list. It is relatively easy to decide to make resolutions as to how you are going to change and what you want to achieve by that change. It is equally easy to break such resolutions!
   You may wish to find time to:

○ *learn to tapdance;*
○ *master your company's squash ladder;*
○ *brush up your German to a level that will boost your career;*
○ *train for a marathon;*
○ *or read some of those management tomes which have been gathering dust on your shelves!*

Such activities should be achievable for you, at least to some degree.

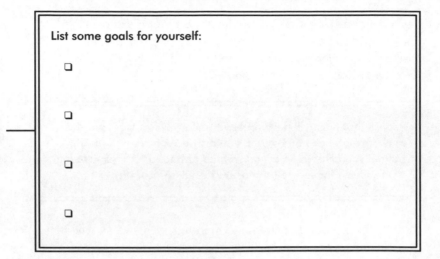

List some goals for yourself:

❑

❑

❑

❑

The reality is that you must be determined to gain control of your life. What are the major hurdles you must clear before you can start to spend more of your time as you wish to?

They might be:

○ *never having a clear desk;*
○ *always being interrupted;*
○ *not believing that those around you can help;*
○ *not saying "no" to work.*

Do any of these sound familiar?

We will discover some techniques to overcome these problems later in the book – at this stage it is just a matter of identifying where you are falling down.

Think of some of your own hurdles. You must understand what they are before you can leap them.

❑

❑

❑

How to improve your understanding of time

The essential first step in mastering your time is to know its value and find where you are frittering it away.

Here's what to do.

1. Time is money – make sure that you are giving value for money to yourself and your company.
2. Accept that there is only one chance to achieve what you want in life so you'd better start now.
3. Analyse your day to see where the time goes. Look for "slack" which could be snatched back for you.
4. Identify ways in which you would rather use your time.
5. Make achievable resolutions to change the way you are going to spend your time.

You should now have appreciated the fact that your time is valuable and have some ideas of what you would rather be doing with it.

What's in this chapter for you

Starting to structure your day
Get the real picture rather than what you imagine
Gather the clues to help you change things
Time thieves

❝ *Time and money are precious resources and few people striving
for success ever believe they possess either one in excess.* ❞
– Napoleon Hill, personal development guru

Most time management theories tell you to keep some kind of a
diary to see how you actually spend your time. The trouble with
this kind of advice is that nobody really follows it! People who can
complete the diary – perfectly tracking every 15 minutes – should
not have a problem with managing their time. Either that or they
are achieving little else in their day except filling out their diaries!

Dissect a typical day

The best way to see what happens to your time is to make a list of
what you do in an average day and add up the time you spend
on each activity. You can fill it in retrospectively.

> Create a chart of your time usage. Divide all your activity at
> work into rough percentages. Be honest with yourself!

Assume, for instance, you are starting work at 9.00 a.m. and
leaving at 5.00 p.m., with a one-hour commute at either end
(and that you're lucky enough to get an hour for lunch!).Your
working day may look something like this:

Commuting	2 hours	20%
Telephone calls	1 hour	10%
Meetings – formal	1.5 hours	15%
Meetings – informal	30 minutes	5%
Waiting between meetings	30 minutes	5%
Networking	30 minutes	5%

Lunch	1 hour	10%
Finding information	1 hour	10%
Writing/dictating	1 hour	10%
Reading reports	1 hour	10%

Even if your list looks entirely different to this, the real point is to identify time you are unhappy about wasting. Lunch in the canteen at work may be important for you socially, but once a week you might want to be doing something else.

Mark against your list those chunks of time that you are unhappy about. Think about how you can reduce this time to its bare minimum and set targets for what you would rather be doing with it instead. For example, could you delegate the information gathering and use that time to learn how to use your computer more efficiently?

❝ *The department had a lunch time ritual. We would go to the restaurant together and then after lunch we played cards. After six months of this, I was overweight, permanently tired and not a little bored! I forced myself on at least three days a week to get out of the office. I started playing squash at lunch time or sometimes just went for a walk. The result? I am fitter, slimmer and not being driven by boredom to look for another job!* **❞**
– Nancy Clarke, sales office administrator

Work out the true picture of what you do with your time. Any Surprises? Turn these discrepancies into action plans for change.

Realistic ambition

If you had more time, what would you do with it? Are your ambitions realistic?

❝ I had learnt basic piano when young. I always felt that I was a performer manqué so my New Year's resolution was to find the time to join a blues band. After three practice sessions with some musician friends, I saw that I was simply not good enough. Once this depressing realisation wore off, I re-set my sights, enrolled for piano lessons and practised as often as I could. After a year I was welcomed back into the band with open arms! ❞
– David Haynes, graphic designer

Ambition is a wonderful thing but dealing with endless setbacks can be difficult. Setting your sights too high will lead to more failures than successes. You need successes to keep you motivated. So break large goals into smaller more achievable steps.

You need to set yourself some achievable goals. These should be written down and displayed somewhere where they'll always be visible – the front of your diary, your screensaver, or your office notice board. Make sure they're suitable for public consumption – "Amputate boss' tongue" is not really an appropriate goal for display in three-foot high letters on your office wall!

You should review this list regularly and measure any achievements against it.

Achievable goals might include:

- *getting fitter by jogging at lunchtimes;*
- *setting up regular informal meetings with colleagues to exchange ideas;*
- *learning to use that new software package;*
- *reading the technical journals you never seem to be able to shift from your pending mountain.*

The Pareto Principle

Do you achieve 80 per cent of your results in 20 per cent of the time you put in?

❝ Phone, pointless meeting, phone, phone, phone – then it's 5.30. I have barely scratched the surface of the work. Then the life-wasters go home and I'm left in peace. In the next two hours, I tear through the in-tray and get it off to the printers. I get most of a full day's work done in just two quiet hours. ❞
– Lawrence Turk, production editor

This phenomenon is called the Pareto Principle. It applies to most people and most companies and suggests that time is not being spent on the correct priorities.

> **If this is how your days pan out, then you need to try to redress the balance.**
>
> ❑ *Identify your objectives and concentrate on the critical ones.*
> ❑ *Stop yourself wasting time on trivia.*
> ❑ *Say "no" to tasks which aren't your immediate concern.*
> ❑ *Learn to delegate at the right times.*
> ❑ *Develop efficient methods at work by analysing what happens to your day.*

There are specific tactics throughout this book to help you break the stranglehold that is the Pareto Principle.

Free lunches

"There is no such thing as a free lunch" is a phrase which is often used to emphasise the importance of valuing time.

> **The real price you pay by accepting a free lunch is the demand on your time. If someone offers to buy you lunch, you sacrifice something – the ability to do something else instead.**

> **❝** *When I first joined the company, my equivalent in marketing, who had been there a long time, kept insisting that we lunch together, often as much as once a week! After three of these lunches, I realised that he was simply wanting to pick my brains and generate some new ideas for his department. The next time he asked, I politely but firmly declined – my lunch time is now my own, to work through or to relax in as I see fit.* **❞**
> **Susanne Hopper, personnel manager**

Next time a free lunch presents itself, ask yourself:

- ○ *"What will I be passing up as a consequence?"*
- ○ *"Is there a hidden agenda?"*
- ○ *"Are they trying to sell me something?"*
- ○ *"Do they want information?"*
- ○ *"Am I going to be bored rigid?"*

If you are hungry and you can see that there's something constructive in it for you, by all means accept. (Constructive does not mean that the offer entails a visit to that little Italian place you'd wanted to check out!) The important thing is to weigh up the cost to you of losing that time.

Do not worry about giving offence by declining calls upon you time – your first priority is to be in control of your own day. If you say "no" in an assertive way, your refusal will soon be forgotten.

Even if you never return the favour, the free lunch will mean some degree of sacrifice. You may simply be on a diet and the last thing you need is the temptation of a calorie loaded menu!
Again, think what could you be doing instead. You could be:

- ○ *working to clear a backlog that's threatening your plan to leave early on Friday;*
- ○ *researching the best deal on your holiday and saving yourself hundreds of pounds;*
- ○ *sticking to the exercise programme you've started;*
- ○ *spending the time with someone more interesting;*
- ○ *dreaming about amputating your boss' tongue!*

Get the idea? Everything you do involves not doing something else. Economists call this concept "opportunity cost".

> **"** *The first time I heard about 'opportunity cost', during a rather dull college lecture, my view of life was instantly changed. It gave me a completely new way of evaluating what I was doing. I realised that my study trips to the library were always interrupted by friends who diverted me from what I needed to do. I developed new studying techniques and ended up with a first class degree.* **"**
> **– Mary Connaught (BA Hons), senior fund manager**

Do you always seem to be thinking that you'd rather be doing something else instead? Work out what is really stopping you, as everything and anything can be changed.

Understand where all of your time goes

The key to changing your routine is to know where you are wasting time unnecessarily.

Here's what to do.

1. Work out and write down where your time is going during the day.
2. Identify where you can make savings and decide what you'd rather be doing with that time.
3. Put your ambitions right at the top of your personal agenda.
4. Set yourself realistic targets in your quest for change – goals that can be achieved gradually and then built on.
5. Decide to change right now – there's no time like the present.
6. Live the concept of "opportunity cost" – always look at what you could be doing instead.
7. Recognise the drain on your time caused by other people. Should you be more assertive?

Once you have identified your squandered time, you can aim at replacing it with activities which are more valuable to you.

What's in this chapter for you

Understanding why you miss deadlines
Beat procrastination – now!
Overcoming fear
The power of positive thinking

> **"** *Some mornings, I find myself walking around my office looking at the piles of work that I must do today. I can't seem to start one task without dropping it because I've started worrying about one of the others.* **"**
> **– Simon Armstrong, freelance editor**

Do you seem to put off doing some daunting tasks rather than getting straight down to them? Do you feel anxious and stressed as a result? Do you seem to fall short of the standards you set for yourself?

Time cancer

There is one word that sums up the major problem that most people have with achieving what they need to . . . *procrastination*. It has an innocent enough ring to it, but it should be as alarming as the word *cancer*.

Definitions first: "procrastinate . . . to put off or defer (an action) to a later time; delay" (*Collins English Dictionary*).

Procrastination is the wasting disease of time. At best it will merely enslave you and force you to squander your days. At worst it will stop you in your tracks. It will freeze your ambitions, handicap you at work and keep you under-achieving.

> ❝ *I had been promoted to sales director; I was confident in my abilities in all areas, except in the financial planning aspects of the job. I hated preparing the budgets, and I would find any excuse to avoid doing them. One year, on the pretext that I was too busy with an overseas subsidiary, I even persuaded the finance director to prepare them for me, based on gibberish I'd dreamt up in a brainstorming session with my reps! It seemed like a great idea at the time, but it soon became obvious that not only were we going to be miles off target but we were also working to a totally unrealistic budget. As a result, I very nearly lost my job.* ❞
> **Adrian Phillips, sales director**

Procrastination really is the major block. Let's break it down into something tangible and recognisable.

> **Do any of these thoughts ring a bell?**
>
> ❏ *"I am not sure how to do this."*
> ❏ *"I'll do the report next week . . ."*
> ❏ *"I'll delay the meeting."*
> ❏ *"I won't discuss their poor time-keeping until next week."*
> ❏ *"That job is just too big and tortuous to look at now."*
> ❏ *"What if I get it wrong?"*

What are you really saying in these circumstances? Quite simply, you are avoiding doing something which you dislike, find boring or awkward, or maybe even think that you cannot do.

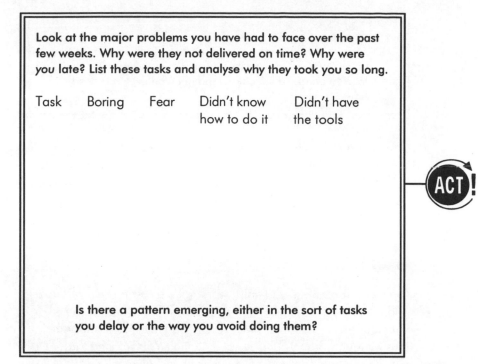

Look at the major problems you have had to face over the past
few weeks. Why were they not delivered on time? Why were
you late? List these tasks and analyse why they took you so long.

Task	Boring	Fear	Didn't know how to do it	Didn't have the tools

**Is there a pattern emerging, either in the sort of tasks
you delay or the way you avoid doing them?**

Classifying your procrastination style is an important step in being
able to move on to greater effectiveness. Something is blocking
your success – it's you and your emotions.

Be honest with yourself. Admit to procrastination then work out
what you're avoiding and why. (Do this now, not tomorrow!)

You should now have a better idea why things do not get done or
done on time. Here are some practical tips as to how to start
meeting your deadlines

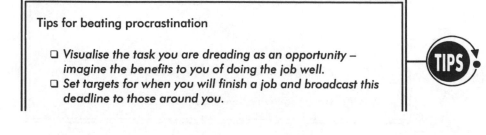

Tips for beating procrastination

- ❑ *Visualise the task you are dreading as an opportunity –
  imagine the benefits to you of doing the job well.*
- ❑ *Set targets for when you will finish a job and broadcast this
  deadline to those around you.*

- *Promise yourself a reward for getting that dreaded job done.*
- *Make a start as soon as you can. Do not allow yourself to delay because you don't yet have all the information or the tools to hand – think ahead and get whatever you need in advance.*

> ❝ *It was obvious that unless I came to grips with my poor financial management, I would not be in the job for long. I spoke to my boss who readily agreed to send me on an intensive training course. It was hard work but it gave me all the confidence I needed to master the financial part of my job.* ❞
> **– Adrian Phillips**

Write lists

Every evening before you finish work, take a clean sheet of paper and jot down the things you aim to have finished by the same time tomorrow. You might wish to highlight the more important jobs although, frankly, this is not essential. You will find that picking off the easier tasks to begin with will give you a psychological boost as you cross them off the list. This will motivate you to start some of the more daunting tasks.

Start on your "to do" list first thing in the morning. Begin with the most palatable and strike them off in a flamboyant fashion to hype yourself up. If possible, break down the longer jobs into more manageable smaller tasks.

The fear factor

Fear is one of the major causes of procrastination.

Is this you?

- *"The report is difficult – what if it's not up to standard?"*
- *"I can't apply for that job – what if I embarrass myself at the interview?"*
- *"OK, I am good in interviews, but what if I can't do the job?"*

I always wanted to try selling as a career. However, I never had the courage to apply for jobs. What if I was no good at it? What would everyone think? **99**
Valerie Miller, former secretary

We all experience fear – that dread of the unknown. In the frantic modern world, however, there really isn't that much to be frightened of – we're all having to deal with change and uncertainty. You aren't alone. By addressing your fears head on, you will find you can make them disappear.

66 *I nearly lost my job because of taking so long to finish tasks. I would check over and over my work, eliminating any chance of mistakes. I fell into the trap of expecting everything I did to be absolutely perfect. I almost achieved this, but then my problem was I'd become far and away the least productive member of our team.* **99**
– Rina Strong, dental laboratory technician

Are the standards you set for yourself too high? Re-set them to be motivating rather than depressing. Be kind to yourself.

Fear of Success

There are two extremes of the fear related to procrastination, fear of failure and fear of success. To fear success may seem somewhat contrary and yet it is still a main reason why people procrastinate.

Do you delay doing things for fear of the consequences? Is it the prospect of further responsibilities or further risks that is holding you back? Will it mean promotion? If you succeed, do you fear that you'll have to tackle more difficult work you have never done before?

❝ Eventually, I took the plunge and, with some trepidation, applied for the sales job. I got it! I've since been promoted twice and am beginning to hanker after a sales director's job. I'd be nervous about the leap, but I know now that I can achieve if I have the courage to try. ❞
– Valerie Miller, sales manager

> **Tips on overcoming fear**
>
> ❑ *Keep telling yourself before you start that you can and will be successful – sooner or later you'll believe it!*
> ❑ *Think back to past achievements and remember the fears you felt before you reached that goal. You did it then – you can do it now!*
> ❑ *View the possibility of failure positively – it's something from which you can learn.*

Remember, the easiest way of overcoming your fears is to think positively.

Positive thinking

If you always take a dim view of youself, it's time to start modifying your thought processes.

❝ I was headhunted by the biggest and most successful of the companies in my field. Within three months of being there, I realised I'd made the worst mistake of my life. The people I worked with were institutionalised (or should have been!), creativity was stifled and I had absolutely no respect for my director. I tried over the months to undermine the corporate ethos. This ended up in my very nearly being sacked after the most damning and (I thought) unjustified appraisal of my life. ❞
– David Crainer, former international sales manager

Do you think your way to failure? Do you always blame others when things go wrong? Do you allow past mistakes to fester?

You might think that you are what you are, and it's too late to change. You'd be wrong. Positive thinking **is** something you can learn to do.

Practise thinking positively. Repeat the following phrases to yourself until they become instinctive.

- ❑ *"This time I'll get it right."*
- ❑ *"How will I stop that happening again?"*
- ❑ *"Next time I'll know what to expect."*
- ❑ *"I CAN do it."*

❝ *I played the game for six months, all the time planning my escape. I left and set up my own business which went well virtually from the start. However, I could not stop myself being eaten up by anger at my treatment – how could they behave with so little respect towards me? Only now, much later, have I learnt to take something positive from the experience. I realise that the company culture was bigger than me and I was not right for the company. I can also see that the anger I'd felt could have been self-destructive.* ❞
– David Crainer, self-employed marketing consultant.

Working when the muse is with you – a caveat

You have seen in this chapter some of the main reasons for procrastination. However, you should also accept that certain sorts of tasks can only be achieved when you are mentally fit to face them.

❝ *My difficulty has always been in recognising whether or not I am in the right mood to do certain tasks. Sometimes I have mornings when I can write a dozen letters perfectly without any problems at all. Other times, I sit and look at the screen and nothing comes. I have learnt when this happens to turn my hand to something else – inevitably the mental block goes by the afternoon.* ❞
– Paul Hammond, direct marketing executive

If you find yourself unable to write or think creatively in the hour before the monthly board meeting, then schedule your time differently and do not commit yourself to certain tasks when you know you are going to struggle to do them. Most importantly, remember not to use this as a delaying tactic! If you have to procrastinate consciously, then reschedule that task for another more conducive time and get on with something else. Use the techniques you have learnt in this chapter to ensure you get back to the first job and get it done on time.

How to get it done, now

The old phrase "procrastination is the thief of time" is as true today as it was when it was coined.

Beat procrastination

1. Analyse why, when and how you tend to procrastinate. Once you can recognise the symptoms, you'll have something to work on.
2. Overcome fear with positive thinking. Imagine yourself doing the job well and the benefits it will bring to you. Keep telling yourself "I *can* do it".
3. If neccessary, use fear positively. Imagine the consequences of not getting the job done.
4. Make a things-to-do list at the end of your day and use it as your agenda for the following day. Break tasks down into more manageable chunks whenever possible. As you start the day, pick off the easiest tasks first – crossing them off the list will spur you on to tackle the monsters.
5. Reward yourself for completing something exceedingly tedious. Having a bar of chocolate or a web-surfing session to look forward to will motivate you to keep on plodding through the task at hand.

6. Set deadlines for yourself and reinforce them by telling others when you will have that piece of work finished.
7. Where possible, make a start immediately, even if you do not have everything you may need to finish it.
8. Set yourself realistic standards. Failure can be very demotivating.
9. Revel in past successes to drive you on to new achievements.

Follow these guidelines and you'll banish procrastination from your life for ever.

What's in this chapter for you

> *Managing your boss*
> *Stopping people stopping you*
> *Beating the thieves of time*
> *Organising your environment*
> *Delegating properly*
> *Working smarter, not longer*

Boxer, the horse in George Orwell's novel *Animal Farm* worked hard, harder and more devotedly than any of the other animals. Manipulated by the pigs running the farm, Boxer would respond to pressure by "working harder". The harder he worked, the more work was expected of him. He is last seen on his way to the slaughter house, useless to his new masters except as food.

> **"** *At every assessment I've had, I was praised for my conscientiousness. No matter what came up in the department, I would offer to do it. I stayed at work late; when security asked me to leave I took work home. The more I did, the more was piled on to me. Eventually, when my health and marriage began to suffer, I realised that I needed to change my approach drastically.* **"**
> **– Kathy Roy, healthcare manager**

Do you ever get the feeling that the more you do, the more you are expected to do? Is working harder and longer proving counter-productive?

Define what is expected of you

Most people have experienced the effect of bad management. The boss is always in a panic, he is blaming downward pressure from his boss and everything ends up getting dumped on your desk to be sorted out immediately.

If you are the sort of person who is accommodating, you may be seen as a "soft touch". You need to learn to define the boundaries within which you are expected to work. Here are some tactics you can use to do this.

○ *If something is dumped on you at short notice, establish the real urgency of the job.*
○ *Given that a job is urgent, does it really need to be done in great depth and detail. Will notes or a précis suffice?*
○ *Reschedule your other work and make your boss aware that certain things will have to slip.*
○ *If your boss is always springing deadlines on you, organise regular short meetings to enable you to plan accordingly and demonstrate that there is too much to do so slippage is inevitable.*
○ *Try to take control of scheduling and work flow wherever possible.*

Homework

Sometimes it will be necessary to take work home. Depending on your circumstances this may be a simple fact of life.

However, you should not get locked into this syndrome. It should be treated as something you are prepared to do in exceptional circumstances but not as a matter of course. Doing it regularly will prove counter-productive in the end as you will pile more and more work and pressure upon yourself and become increasingly stressed out.

> **❝** *Parkinson's Law states that work expands to fill the time available. By increasing the hours I was prepared to work, I was also simply dragging out my current workload unnecessarily and therefore working less efficiently. And, worse, it encouraged the others to dump even more work on me.* **❞**
> **– Kathy Roy**

What is working long hours doing to you physically and mentally. Are your relationships suffering as a result? Is this a price that it is really worth paying?

Very often people who take work home don't actually do anything with it. Taking work home may make being at work marginally more tolerable in the short term but it will just mess up your home life.

> Wherever possible avoid taking work home – try to finish it in the office, the pressure will make you more efficient. Should you have to, do not make a habit of it!

❝ My first managerial job was in a company that had an approach to time management that was pure machismo. You were perceived as a wimp if you weren't working a ten hour day. I was never convinced that this supposed dedication was anything other than posturing on the part of the management. I had young children that I was not seeing all week. After six months, I started to keep sensible hours by working efficiently during the day and letting others know it. Interestingly, when I bucked the trend, others followed! ❞
– Steve Cawthorne, production manager

Hell is other people

You should now decide to look at your working day and where the hours are going.

Which of the following are relevant to your average day:

- ❑ *you spend hours in meetings;*
- ❑ *the telephone keeps interrupting you;*
- ❑ *you see too many unexpected visitors;*
- ❑ *you cannot seem to delegate effectively.*

What is happening here? Quite simply, other people are making their demands on your time at the expense of your own. Let's look at these demands on an individual basis.

Meetings

Companies worldwide waste millions with the "what shall we do now? – let's have a meeting!" syndrome. But how productive are the meetings that you regularly attend?

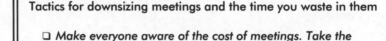

❝ I had a monthly meeting some 60 miles away at head office. I knew that these were ultimately a waste of my time but the ritual had been set long ago. I decided to break the mould. I cancelled one meeting at short notice, having made an appointment with a key customer for the same time. I asked for the minutes, worked through them and sent in my thoughts and comments. For the next meeting, I sent my assistant, having primed him beforehand. It ended up that I only attended four such meetings a year. Others managers began to follow suit, and eventually the meetings became quarterly events. ❞
– Susan Hillier, sales manager

If your company is riddled with meetings which are difficult to avoid then you should take the initiative and try to weed out as many as possible. If some meetings are the cherished territory of senior managers, try to cut yourself out.

Tactics for downsizing meetings and the time you waste in them

❏ *Make everyone aware of the cost of meetings. Take the hourly average salary of those attending, multiply it by the time spent annually at such events and circulate the total cost. This should have the effect of reducing wastage!*
❏ *Chase the agenda to ensure it is set well beforehand and circulated. The agenda should be stuck to rigidly – politely but firmly use it as a tool to stop people with a tendency to waffle.*
❏ *Ensure that the meeting is properly chaired. If necessary, chair it yourself!*
❏ *Use new technology to avoid face-to-face meetings wherever possible. Can the same results be gained by teleconferencing? Can E-mail help to disseminate information?*
❏ *Wherever possible, send a deputy to the slaughter!*

Telephone techniques

❝ My northern agent would faithfully phone me weekly, as he was meant to, in order to give me brief details of the market in his area. What should have been a 10 minute conversation always ended up

taking 45 minutes and, as I was new to the job, I felt I was being terribly supportive by listening. However, after one such conversation when he spent 15 minutes telling me about the family problems of one of his key customers, I knew that this had to be stopped. In future when he phoned, I would say to him that I had only 10 minutes so he had to keep it brief – anything that needed more detail should be put in memo form which I could then get my assistant to answer. **99**

– Tracey Rodgers, area manager.

Telephones are a wonderful invention but they can be voracious users of time. Avoiding wastage is an essential part of clawing back time to use on something else.

Taming your telephone time

❑ *Use an answerphone or voice mail when you do not want to be interrupted. If possible, delegate the job of answering to someone else.*
❑ *If you regularly find yourself taking messages for someone else, explain politely the costs in time this involves for you. Suggest they use an answerphone or voice mail!*
❑ *Conversations with pathologically garrulous people should always start by you defining how much time you can spare. Try to get them to do the speaking (which shouldn't be difficult). Give only yes/no responses – chipping in with relevant personal anecdotes will only prolong the whole thing.*
❑ *Before making a call, set your own agenda and stick to it!*

Unexpected guests

66 *I firmly believed that managers should be accessible at all times. My door was always open and anyone walking in would get a welcoming smile. I found myself listening to office gossip and personal gripes all of the time.* **99**

– Angela Niven, customer services manager

Available to help in problem-solving – yes. Willing to watch the sands of your life seeping through your fingers as you suffer at the mouth of yet another carping nerd – no! It's your time being stolen.

You should aim to be accessible to the people around you, but on your own terms. Do not be aloof, but make it absolutely clear when you are willing to see people.

Dealing with "visitors" on your terms

❏ *If you do not want to be disturbed, shut the door or, in an open-plan office, face away from the point of access.*
❏ *Agree signals with your colleagues that they all understand and stick to. For example, hanging your jacket on the back of your chair could mean that you are not to be disturbed, unless it's news of your Lottery win!*
❏ *If you are asked whether you're free and you are not, politely but firmly say so and set another time.*
❏ *Use body language – if someone comes in unexpectedly, stand up, look them in the eye and make it plain that now is not the right time. Do not give them the opportunity to sit down – remove extra chairs beforehand if you want.*
❏ *Say straight away that you're too busy, and that you'll come to them as soon as you can. It's easier to leave their workspace than to get them out of yours.*

Delegating, not passing the buck

Are you paranoid that if you pass on a task to someone else, it will not be done well and will reflect badly on you? This is a commmon fear that stops people delegating effectively. There are many others:

○ *"Somebody else will steal my thunder."*
○ *"I need to know what's going on, no matter how trivial."*
○ *"I quite enjoy taking time out to do some easy tasks."*
○ *"My boss will think I'm dispensable."*
○ *"It's quicker to do it myself than explain it."*
○ *"I'll be told to clear off and it could lead to a scene."*

Delegation is a difficult skill to master. However, you can learn some basic rules right away.

We have already looked at the economic value of your time and this is the starting point when considering what to delegate.

Are you really being paid to undertake all the tasks you are currently doing. Could someone else do them more cost-effectively?

> **❝** *I am aware that working out monthly commission payments for my sales team takes up a lot of my time. But it's complicated and it would take me ages to explain what to do and then check the figures. I might as well do it myself.* **❞**
> **– Steve Wilson, accounts manager**

Tips on successful delegation

- ❑ *Delegate the right work – analyse every task that you do and be certain that you are the person who should be doing it.*
- ❑ *Empower those around you – appreciate the talents of others, accept that they need new challenges and learn to trust their abilities.*
- ❑ *Select the right person for the job – someone that will see the new task as a worthwhile challenge.*
- ❑ *Don't give the impression that you are "dumping" your work – present new tasks to people as a sign of your trust in their abilities. Make it positive!*
- ❑ *Give a full brief – spend time explaining the job in detail and ensure that your delegates know what to do right from the start.*
- ❑ *In the early stages, check their progress regularly – this will save you having to re-do the job and save them the embarrassment of watching you freak out.*
- ❑ *Be effusive with your praise when a job is well done – it will make it easier to delegate in future and encourages the recipients to accept.*
- ❑ *Above all, do not see it as a threat!*

Learning effective delegation is not something you will achieve overnight. It needs to be worked at constantly as it is inevitably tied in with your relationships with those around you. However, you must start applying some of the techniques discussed here if you are really serious about improving your efficiency at work.

If you are lucky enough to have secretarial support, make sure that those people know your priorities. Not only should you be delegating a lot of routine tasks to them, but you can also use them to shield you from time-wasters. To do this you must ensure you fully empower them.

Tips on saving time at work

If you fully understand the causes of your lost time at work, it should be possible for you to make savings.

How to save time at work

1. Do not accept that those above you have a God-given right to involve you in their fire-fighting by springing work on you. Drag them back into the fray by asking them to choose what to drop from the list of tasks that can no longer be done during the working day.
2. Treat taking work home with you as the exception, not the rule. If you don't, you'll clutter your personal life as well.
3. Break the mould of macho corporate cultures and their demands on your time. Set your sights on working effectively so you can arrive and leave on time.
4. Control the length of telephone calls by setting time limits. Tell chatter addicts right at the start that you only have 5 minutes to spare, and stick to what you've said.
5. Cost the value of meetings. Putting things in money terms can give you a powerful argument for dropping meetings that waste your time.
6. Ensure that meetings are run to time – chair them yourself if necessary! Make sure that the agenda is circulated well before the meeting and, if possible, resolve some of the issues in advance.
7. Do not hold or attend meetings for the sake of them. And, if you can, send somebody in your place.

8. Only allow people access to you on your terms. If you are too busy, say so and fix another time. If you need to, see people in their work space – it's easier to escape from their space than to get them out of your office.

9. Delegate effectively – that is, delegate to the right people for the right reasons. Make sure you fully brief them and check their work thoroughly in the early stages. The job will soon be getting done all by itself, leaving you free to do something else.

Now that you know how to cut down the time-wasting, you'll see your efficiency grow steadily.

What's in this chapter for you

Organising your working environment
Setting priorities
Planning your time
Developing speed skills
Managing the information flow
Filling in dead time
Saving time with technology

In the last chapter we looked at the negative effect other people can have on your use of time. But look around you. Are your own weaknesses holding you back? And, are you giving the right impression?

> Do you have the necessary practical systems in place to manage your working environment? Is your workspace conducive to being efficient? Is it you rather than others who are wasting time?

> 〝 *I dearly wanted to be able to deal with the sheer volume of work that crossed my desk every day, but I never knew where to start. Despite my best intentions, it just kept building up and I constantly felt like I was drowning in it. It was incredibly stressful.* 〞
> **– Karen Stark, credit controller**

Let's start by dealing with the paperwork.

Setting priorities

Most of us are swamped with constant streams of paperwork. Devising efficient ways to deal with it all is fundamental to maximising your use of time.

> You should if possible delegate the task of filtering your mail daily so that the obvious rubbish is binned and items not for you are distributed to the right people.

There are broad categories into which most tasks fall. The following scale can be used to plot nearly everything that you do.

(1) Urgent/Important

- *Any task that must be done today – by you alone!*
- *Failing to do it could have untold repercussions for you.*
- *Such tasks must be given top priority.*

(2) Urgent/Non Important

- *This is work which needs to be dealt with today.*
- *It should only take up a small amount of your valuable time.*
- *It can be delegated.*

(3) Non-urgent/Important

- *Ongoing projects which need to be completed but with no immediate deadline.*
- *You can re-schedule these tasks to a more convenient time.*
- *Warning! Work in this area may need to be re-categorised as Urgent/Important should the deadline creep up on you.*
- *Warning! Do not treat work in this section as an excuse to procrastinate.*

(4) Non-Urgent/Non-Important

- *These are routine tasks, such as archiving files or reading circulars, everyday reports and trade journals.*
- *The majority of this work can be delegated – or binned!*
- *If you feel you have to, carry this work with you and do it during dead time, such as in the car between appointments (when parked, obviously!) or on the train while commuting.*
- *These tasks are rarely job-threatening.*

It should be possible to categorise most of your work in this way. It may be that some tasks are quite marginal. Other decisions may be straightforward except that you distort the perceptions of what is important. This can be checked out with the people you work with or your boss.

Analyse the kind of things that hit your desk regularly and allocate each to the correct category. Now, look at your current workload. Have you a stack of Urgent/Important tasks piling up and threatening to overwhelm you? Get started on them right away!

You may also use this system as a template for your "to do" list which we talked about earlier. If you do, the category 1 jobs should be right at the top of the list. However, you could also implement this method by having four folders, marked accordingly, into which you place relevant tasks. You can then work through them systematically, ensuring you begin with at least some of level 1 jobs.

> ❝ *By starting the most important jobs first, and recognising the priorities, I no longer feel that I'm drowning.* ❞
> **Karen Stark**

Be ruthless. Use the above system to categorise everything. If it's Urgent/Important, start it now. If it's Urgent/Non-important, make sure you have the time to tackle it today or delegate it. If it's Non-urgent/Important, be aware of looming deadlines and plan a realistic start date – stick to it. As for the rest, get it filed or dump it.

Just-in-case hoarding

So many people keep useless paper because one day "it may prove useful". This may be fine, but don't let it get in the way of what's really important!

Don't let the paperwork get on top of you if you are hoarder. If you must keep things, look carefully at what you do with them. Here are some tips.

- ⭘ *Letters – ensure only one copy is filed. If it is copied from someone else, read then bin it.*
- ⭘ *Computer reports – file centrally in appropriate folders. Do not pile them up on the floor. If you can access the same information on*

the screen yourself, aks why you are receiving printouts in the first place.
- ○ Trade magazines – annotate them as they arrive and keep only the last six months' issues. Clear out the old ones, ripping out or copying any important articles and filing them.
- ○ Scraps of paper, post-it notes – use for note-taking only. Immediately transfer any information on them into a note book or address book and then bin them!
- ○ Months' worth of minutes of regular meetings – bin them! They should be being updated on an ongoing basis.
- ○ If you're a collector of business cards, buy an appropriate holder and use it properly – remember, there's little point in keeping people's cards if they've long since moved on!

Your desk

> **❝** *I could never be accused of being tidy! My desk always looks like it's been bombed – piles of paper everywhere. My colleagues always joked about it, and I always prided myself on the fact that I could find important documents (eventually!), but the new boss has been very critical of the image I give off. He seems to be under the impression that it is not what you do but how you are seen to be doing it which is important.* **❞**
> **– Louise Bentley, financial controller**

Treat your desk as the most valuable ally you have. Here are some features you'll find on a well-organised desk.

- ○ Pen and paper to hand. Write notes down as discussions happen and add these to your daily list of things to do if they are important. If you have a sudden unrelated flash of inspiration while doing something else, write it down. Otherwise, it will disappear into the ether.
- ○ In-tray kept tidy and well structured, not a dumping ground for that 1976 report on pigeon breeding in Finland which you thought might be useful in the future.
- ○ Diary/personal organiser. Have it to hand always to arrange meetings (or to find excuses for not attending!).
- ○ Computer – if you need one on the desk, ensure it is within easy reach so that you do not have to stretch uncomfortably to use it. Make sure that the wires are tucked away neatly – electrocuting your staff will make the process of delegation much more difficult.
- ○ The all-important telephone – this should be positioned by your non-dominant hand. When it rings you should be able to pick it up and take notes almost immediately.

○ *Try to keep staplers, calculators etc. off the desk surface. Put them in a top drawer where they can be reached easily but do not create clutter.*

Like it or not, your desk says a lot about you and your efficiency. Teetering piles of papers, files and printouts might enhance your self-image as an overworked interesting Bohemian sort of character, but it will probably suggest to your boss that you are wildly inefficient and to your staff that they are working for someone with no right to criticise their efficiency at the next appraisal. Either way, what you are losing is respect from all sides.

If you are at one with your desk, you'll find it easier to cope with your workload. Any time you invest in desk organisation will be repaid many fold.

Managing information

" *I seem to have thousands of papers, reports and journals crossing my desk every week. I know that I have to absorb them to stay abreast of current trends but, if I did that, I couldn't do the job I'm paid for.* "
Kevin Barnes, software developer

Information dominates working life. Keeping on top of reading material and other media is important to your success. You need to appraise the ways in which you use information.

Reading is still the main way most of us process information. Work out the system by which you identify what to read and what to ignore.

Contrary to popular belief, it is possible to learn to read in different ways according to the demands of the document concerned.

○ *"Speed reading" is essential when you need to get a quick overall picture of what is being discussed. It involves centring your vision* on the page and reading down. Practise this – you will be surprised at how much information you can absorb in a relatively short space of time.

○ *"Skim reading"* is best achieved by reading down and across the page and skipping certain groups of words and even whole sentences. This method can be particularly useful if the originator of the text can be persuaded to highlight the central points first.

○ *"Detail reading"* is used where an understanding of every word, sentence and nuance is essential – for instance, when studying contracts or anything legal. You might need to make appropriate notes as you read in case you need to go back over certain points.

○ *"Leisure reading"*, as it suggests, is more likely to be used when reading a novel for enjoyment – this method has no fixed rules since it is entirely subjective and rarely has any relevance at work (unless your next promotion depends on your knowledge of the latest offering from Barbara Cartland).

❝ *Once I discovered how to skim read, I found I could extract the most salient points quickly. I now feel I'm up to date and on top of my work.* ❞

Kevin Barnes

Do you get regular reports circulated which are overly long and very boring? If so, apply the appropriate reading method – or, better still, get the author to attach a "key points" précis.

Do you need a reading material tray to stack up the incoming information? If so, make sure it's not on your precious desk and be ruthless. Throw things away that don't need a second look and keep only what is important. Books were once sacred and precious objects. Now they are just tools to help you be more effective so treat them as such. If you own the book, highlight the most relevant points to you.

Effective writing

Never mind the quality feel the width is a prevalent attitude when it comes to writing styles in most organisations. This wastes time for you writing and for those reading.

❝ My boss was a report freak. He conjured up a 200-pager to detail a customer's needs. It was so inpenetrable that everybody in the team missed a crucial part of the specification. We almost supplied exactly what the customer didn't want and wasted huge sums back-tracking. He's not my boss any more! ❞
Steve Marshall, systems designer

Remember, a report does not have to be long to be good.

- ❑ *Limit whenever possible the amount that you write and concentrate on providing easy-to-read chunks of information.*
- ❑ *For complicated reports, give a summary of the issues which can be readily absorbed.*

Not only is brevity essential in communicating information, it also plays an important part in recording it. Imagine yourself being briefed by a customer who is pouring out facts which you need to take in at the same time as responding appropriately. Can you take them all down quickly enough?

If you are making notes at a meeting , develop your own shorthand systems. Or, rather, If mkng nts, dvp yr own s/h syst. Get the picture?

Filling in the gaps

❝ My new job meant three hours a day commuting in the car. When I started, I tried to educate myself by listening to classical music and even bought some language tapes. That lasted three weeks. I now have an encyclopaedic knowledge of contemporary pop music and trivia which enhances my street credibility with my children. However, it is an appalling waste of time. ❞
Mark Burton, product manager

Commuting by car, or driving between appointments is an unfortunate fact of life for many people. It is not feasible to suggest that every second should be used improving one's mind –

we all have to relax and switch off occasionally. However, you can productively fill in the gaps of your day which would be otherwise wasted.

How often do you turn up for an appointment half an hour early because traffic conditions make it impossible to be accurate about your time of arrival?

Here are some tips on how to constructively fill those gaps.

Make use of dead time

- ❏ *Remember those important but non-urgent reports you should read? Don't leave them in the office – take a pile out with you on a trip to read in the car between appointments.*
- ❏ *Always have a dictaphone with you. You can use this to dictate reports and letters, record your ideas as they occur and build up your "to do" list for the next day.*
- ❏ *Invest in a mobile phone – you can get many of the routine calls you need to make out of the way in otherwise dead time. You can also ring the person you are due to see to check that they are there and avoid the possibilty of making wasted journey.*
- ❏ *Sit and think! This does not mean dreaming about your forthcoming summer holiday or the next round of golf you will play. Take time out of the office to think strategically, analyse ongoing problems or to concoct some creative copy (use that dictaphone!).*

Time-saving technology

The range of computer software and other technological gadgets seems to be growing exponentially at the moment and the list of features on offer is bewildering. To deal with this, you must convince yourself that technology is there to help you.

There are some simple rules for dealing with the high-tech world.

- ❑ *Know exactly what you want it to do and why. Don't buy anything until you've had a convincing demonstration that this is the gizmo for you.*
- ❑ *Get a support agreement from whomever sells to you. You'll need to be shown exactly how to use it and have somebody to call if it goes wrong.*
- ❑ *Don't waste time trying to solve problems. Ask somebody else. More often than not they'll glow with pride if they can casually show you where to click and what to push.*
- ❑ *Find out what can and can't be done with the equipment you have at your disposal. Again, you'll save time if you simply ask other people.*

TIPS

> ❝ *I've always been bad at maths. I used to fumble around with a calculator and an overhead projector at sales meetings, looking like the court jester. God knows how I kept my job! Now I've got a laptop computer. All I have to do is punch in the figures and up pops a chart, a graph, whatever. I can play with the figures by asking 'what if?' questions and the display adjusts automatically. My customers think I'm a genius!* ❞
> **Gary Clarke, financial consultant**

Examine carefully what your job entails and identify where technology could speed things up. For instance, if you send out hundreds of standard letters, wordprocessors allow you to create the letter once and then add all the personal details from the database as well as printing the labels. The key is to ask: "what can this box of tricks do for me?" and find somebody who can show you.

Do you have a computer on your desk that you use as nothing more than a glorified typewriter? If you do, invest some time finding out how it could make your life easier.

> ❝ *The boss finally agreed to get us a new computer and the software we wanted. Only one between three of us, mind, but the first step on the road to self-sufficiency. However, the training budget only extended to four hours of the consultant's time and, to save hurt feelings, everybody in the department was invited. Ten people huddled around one computer, the cursor whizzing around, things flashing up, the office half-wit diverting everybody – none of us was any the wiser after our four hours.* ❞
>
> **Mel Winton, editorial assistant**

Lack of training is a common problem. It's often left to the users to "play" with the equipment and learn it themselves. If they are already under pressure, it is unlikely that the system will ever be mastered. This is made worse by justifiable allergic reactions to manuals.

> Make time to experiment with new products. It will pay dividends in the long run. If you can, ask other users to explain the basics to you – an experienced user could probably show you in seconds what you've struggled for hours to fathom with the help (*sic*) of your manual.

> ❝ *Our new system became nothing more than an impressive ornament. It was certainly never used to full effect before I left and yet it's now standard practice in other companies I've visited.* ❞
>
> **Mel Winton**

Although they can't yet wander off and make you a cup of coffee, office computers are now incredibly sophisticated. You can scan in text from printed pages, supply the tax people with your annual return at the press of a button, even dictate a letter (that will be corrected gramatically) directly on to the screen. An electronic organiser can replace your address book, calculator, diary, notepad and alarm clock, and yet fit in your shirt pocket.

By analysing your needs and finding out what's available, you could save a lot of precious time. Don't be intimidated, investigate.

How to organise your work life

By looking critically at what you do and how you do it, you should see where you could be more efficient and save yourself time.

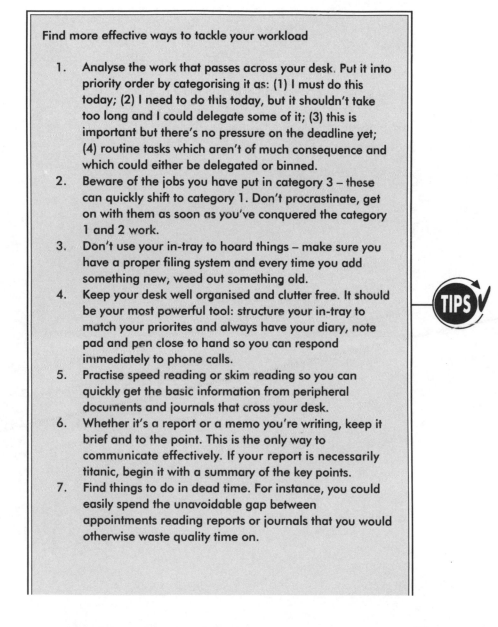

Find more effective ways to tackle your workload

1. Analyse the work that passes across your desk. Put it into priority order by categorising it as: (1) I must do this today; (2) I need to do this today, but it shouldn't take too long and I could delegate some of it; (3) this is important but there's no pressure on the deadline yet; (4) routine tasks which aren't of much consequence and which could either be delegated or binned.

2. Beware of the jobs you have put in category 3 – these can quickly shift to category 1. Don't procrastinate, get on with them as soon as you've conquered the category 1 and 2 work.

3. Don't use your in-tray to hoard things – make sure you have a proper filing system and every time you add something new, weed out something old.

4. Keep your desk well organised and clutter free. It should be your most powerful tool: structure your in-tray to match your priorites and always have your diary, note pad and pen close to hand so you can respond immediately to phone calls.

5. Practise speed reading or skim reading so you can quickly get the basic information from peripheral documents and journals that cross your desk.

6. Whether it's a report or a memo you're writing, keep it brief and to the point. This is the only way to communicate effectively. If your report is necessarily titanic, begin it with a summary of the key points.

7. Find things to do in dead time. For instance, you could easily spend the unavoidable gap between appointments reading reports or journals that you would otherwise waste quality time on.

TIPS ✓

8. Dissect the individual tasks you perform and identify any processes which could be speeded up by using a gadget or some new software. Invest some time finding out what technology is available – it could well reward you with huge savings.

9. Find out the capabilities of the equipment you have. Ask other users. You should try to use it to full effect in the battle to save your time.

If you follow these tips, you should notice a surge in your productivity. By working more efficiently, you'll find your work life more rewarding and your home life more fulfilling.